FOUR AGAINST THE ODDS

The Struggle to Save Our Environment

Stephen
Krensky

SCHOLASTIC INC.
New York Toronto London Auckland Sydney

For Joyce Gregorian Hampshire

Photo Credits

Culver Pictures: p. 4; Los Angeles County Museum of Natural History, History Division: p. 6; Nina Wallace: p. 10; The Kansas State Historical Society, Topeka: p. 15; Culver Pictures: p. 17; Culver Pictures: p. 18; The Sierra Club: p. 20; Culver Pictures: p. 26; Houghton Mifflin: p. 28; The Library of Congress: p. 30; The Bettmann Archive: p. 31; AP/Wide World Photos: p. 43; United Press International Photo: p. 46; Citizens' Clearinghouse for Hazardous Waste: p. 50; Wide World Photos: p. 52; AP Laserphoto: p. 56; AP/Wide World Photos: p. 59; AP/Wide World Photos: p. 64; UPI/Bettmann: p. 67; AP/Wide World Photos: p. 69; AP/Wide World Photos: p. 74; Jim McMahon: p. 76; Nichols/Magnum: p. 78; Brad Hamann: p. 84; JB Pictures: p. 90; JB Pictures: p. 95.

ISBN 0-590-44743-2

12   1 2/0

Printed in the U.S.A.   40

First Scholastic printing, April 1992

Contents

Introduction

Until the 1700s, people did not have a huge impact on nature. For one thing, there were fewer people then. In 1650 the earth's population was only 500 million. (It is more than ten times that today.) For another, nature was still undisturbed in many places. There were large areas of the world where hardly anybody lived.

Pollution was not a big problem, either. People didn't know much about using chemicals. They had few machines to help them work. Blacksmiths were probably among the worst polluters, and they mostly made horseshoes or simple tools.

The Industrial Revolution changed the relationship between people and nature. Technology in the 1800s improved at a fantastic rate. Advances in medicine gave more people longer lives. Advances in science gave these same people more control over their environment. Trains and steam-ships, and later, cars and airplanes, allowed every-one to move about more quickly than before.

Nature couldn't keep up. The old wilderness was vanishing. Natural resources were used up faster than they could be renewed. And the work of en-gines and factories was more than the weather could wipe away.

For a long time, though, people continued to take nature for granted. The four people included here — John Muir, Rachel Carson, Lois Gibbs, and Chico Mendes — did not. They came from dif-ferent times and backgrounds. But they all saw dangers in the way people treated the environ-ment. Each of them tried to make us understand how fragile the environment really is.

The battles they fought were not popular ones, but they fought them, anyway. The stakes were too high to ignore. As Rachel Carson once said, ". . . we have now acquired a fateful power to alter and destroy nature. But man is part of nature and his war against nature is inevitably a war against himself."

John Muir.

JOHN MUIR
Fosters Respect for the Wilderness

The year 1849 will always be remembered for the California Gold Rush. The gold was first discovered in 1848 at Sutter's Mill, near San Francisco, and news of this discovery spread across the country. It was not an ordinary story. The promise of quick riches prompted thousands of people to pack their bags and head west. Some of these hopeful pioneers actually reached California. Others stopped along the way, becoming farmers, ranchers, or tradesmen. Together they helped settle the frontier faster than anyone had expected.

That frontier had grown at an amazing rate. The Louisiana Purchase of 1803 had doubled the size of the young United States. The annexation of Texas in 1845 added more territory. After the end of the Mexican War in 1848, California and most of the Southwest joined the country.

Gold miners in California in the mid-19th century.

These changes took place in a very short time. Such growth gave the nation a feeling of unlimited space. In European countries, every nook and cranny was already spoken for. Americans, however, had more land than they knew what to do with.

Many of the pioneers were looking for a fresh start. Twenty years after the Gold Rush, San Francisco was still a booming town. It was booming so fast that many supplies were scarce. Buildings were constructed from scraps of wood. Nothing was made to last. Fires swept through every so often, burning everything. Still, the rush of people continued. In 1860, the city had boasted a population of 57,000. By 1868 it had doubled that.

Overland travelers to San Francisco came on horses or in wagon trains. (The transcontinental railroad was not yet complete.) From the East

Coast, many passengers preferred the reliable ocean voyage around South America.

One shipboard arrival in March 1868 was a lean man with straggly hair and a bushy beard. He had few belongings besides the clothes on his back. The name and address in his journal read *John Muir, Earth-Planet, Universe.*

Muir's family was from Scotland. They had moved to America in 1849, during the height of the Gold Rush. Muir was eleven then. He had fond memories of the six-week voyage.

> Father and sister Sarah, with most of the old folk, stayed below in rough weather, groaning in the miseries of seasickness . . . But no matter how much the old tub tossed about and battered the waves, we [John and his brother David] were on deck every day, not in the least seasick, watching the sailors at their rope-hauling and climbing work; joining in their songs, learning the names of the ropes and sails, and helping them as far as they would let us . . .

The Muirs had no interest in gold or California. They were heading for a farming life in Wisconsin. That was going to be adventure enough for them.

Farm life had been hard. John's father was a rigid man. He kept them to a demanding schedule. "Excepting Sundays," Muir later wrote, "we boys had only two days of the year to ourselves, the 4th of July and the 1st of January . . . all the others were labor days, rain or shine, cold or warm." Young John rose early each morning to make time to read books. He also enjoyed caring for the animals. He learned "to respect them and love them, and even to win some of their love."

At twenty-two, in 1860, Muir went off to the state university. His father was against the idea and refused to help him. Muir left home with about fifteen dollars in his pocket — all the money he had.

Through the kindness of some professors and students, he was soon comfortably settled. His further schooling went smoothly. Most notably it introduced him to the science of botany. He had always admired flowers and plants. Now he set out to learn about them as well.

At the same time, John showed great promise as an inventor. After leaving college, he took a factory job in Indianapolis, where he worked with machinery for a carriage manufacturer. But an accident there changed his life. A splinter hit his right eye, causing temporary blindness. For weeks he was blind in his left eye, too.

During this time, Muir thought about all the beautiful things he might never see again. When his sight returned, he gave up thoughts of a career in industry. He had always loved the woods. Now, in 1867, he decided to become a naturalist.

He planned a three-year journey of exploration. After that, perhaps, he would settle down. For the moment, he would look no farther than the next hill. With little money, but a strong sense of adventure, he began a thousand-mile walk to Florida.

Muir was not in a hurry. Some days he spent many hours simply admiring a view. Everywhere he went, he studied the trees and flowers in detail.

Along the way, he heard tales of California. These were not tales of its gold or riches; they were tales of its beauty. And the most beautiful place of all was the Yosemite Valley, one hundred miles east of San Francisco.

Muir was determined to see it for himself. It was this wish that had brought him to San Francisco in 1868. He had little interest in the city, though. Cities made him uncomfortable. Muir was eager to stretch his legs. He soon set out for Yosemite.

Yosemite was the name of the Indian tribe who had occupied the land years before. The first mountain men had discovered it in 1833. Even among the breathtaking sights of the West, Yosemite was special. By 1855, sightseers were touring the area. Nine years later, Congress set aside the Yosemite Valley "for public use, resort and recreation . . . for all time." There was not yet any national park system, so California ran Yosemite as a state park.

As always, Muir was traveling lightly. He had a blanket, some flour, and some tea. He wouldn't shoot animals for food. He didn't even carry a gun. He hoped that if he left the bears and mountain lions alone, they would do the same with him.

Among western travelers, he was unusual in other ways as well. Muir did not measure the value of a forest by the lumber it could produce. He did

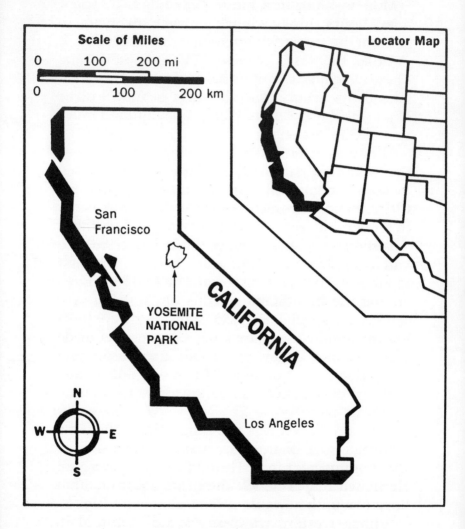

Yosemite National Park

not reckon a mountain's worth by the metal ore lying beneath it. He did not praise a meadow for the heads of livestock that could graze there.

Muir appreciated the wilderness simply for its beauty. He wrote of how "the landscapes of the Santa Clara Valley were fairly drenched with sunshine, all the air was quivering with the songs of the meadowlarks, and the hills were so covered with flowers that they seemed to be painted."

Muir's first look at Yosemite was a dramatic one. It was seven miles long and as much as a mile wide. The trees were tall and majestic, but they were dwarfed by the sheer granite walls rimming the valley. Five waterfalls sent streams of water down their sides. They made rainbows where the spray caught the sunlight.

Muir's trip to Yosemite lasted ten days. Short of money, he then returned to the San Joaquin Valley to find work. He got a job as a shepherd. Muir had never tended sheep before, but he quickly mastered it. The woolly creatures were not very demanding. "Sheep brain," he wrote, "must surely be poor stuff."

The next summer Muir returned to Yosemite. Now he had weeks to enjoy it more fully. Later that fall, he took a job there operating a sawmill. Muir agreed to run it because he still enjoyed tinkering with machinery. But he refused to cut down any live trees.

His first task was to build himself a cabin. It was small and simple with one special feature. Muir dug a ditch to bring a stream under one wall of the cabin. From there it crossed the floor, flowing out under another wall. The cabin was admittedly primitive. But, as he noted, it did have running water.

Muir used all his free time to explore. There was no one to guide him about clothing or equipment. He decided these things for himself. Depending on the weather, he wore several layers of clothing. He avoided coats — they were too difficult to climb in. His shoes were sturdy with thick soles. For instruments he brought a watch, a barometer, and a small magnifying glass to examine plant life.

Muir had no fear of exploring alone. Sometimes he took dangerous chances. He scaled sheer cliffs and mountainsides where no one had gone before. He romped knee-deep in the snow. One day an avalanche almost buried him. He was saved by luck and his ability to ride spread-eagled on top of the rushing snow.

Muir did more than just explore, though. Over the next few years he documented the geology of Yosemite. With scientific precision he charted its natural history. How had the land ended up that way? What forces had been at work? What plants and animals were native to the area? Why did some flourish and others not?

On December 5, 1871, the *New York Tribune* published "Yosemite Glaciers," his first article. His style was direct. His enthusiasm was obvious. Readers could almost see what Muir himself had seen.

The article was popular, and the *Tribune* asked

for more. Muir supplied them. Then, in 1873, he published *Sierra Studies*. It was a larger account of his work. His most important discovery concerned glaciers. They were huge mountains of ice that had moved slowly across the earth during earlier Ice Ages. As the glaciers moved, they carved the ground beneath them. The Great Lakes, for example, were scooped out by glaciers 20,000 years ago.

Muir believed glaciers had formed the Yosemite Valley, too. This view contradicted the accepted scientific opinion of the time. The state geologist of California made fun of Muir for his strange ideas. What did this sheepherder know? It was very clear that the Yosemite Valley had been created by some sort of ancient earthquake or other upheaval.

Muir did not agree, and he continued his research. Eventually he found small living glaciers still at work in the mountains nearby. His documented observations changed the way scientists looked at Yosemite. It also greatly increased his reputation.

At the same time he was becoming more aware of threats to the wilderness. The West was changing. Promoters still hailed it as a place of endless resources. They exaggerated. Many of these resources were already strained. Farmers were fighting over water rights. Cattlemen were elbowing one another for grazing land. Lumberjacks were getting harder pressed to reach uncut forests.

Large and small things troubled Muir in the

woods. He fretted over illegal logging camps, as well as the litter of careless tourists. On February 5, 1875, he wrote an article for the *Sacramento Record-Union*. The great woods were at risk, he stated. The state must more actively manage the forests. Would the state take up this responsibility?

Muir had good reason to wonder. Preserving the wilderness had never been an American priority. Land development had been the key to opening up the West. It served many powerful economic interests.

Lumber, mining, and cattle concerns all owned huge land holdings. But the largest property owners were the railroads. They had acquired this land through the generosity of Congress, which in 1862 authorized the building of a transcontinental railroad. In 1864, the Union Pacific (an eastern railroad) and the Central Pacific (based in California) began working on the project. In return the two companies received land grants (in addition to monetary grants and loans) for every mile of track laid. These two railroads eventually received about 19,000,000 acres of free land. All together, between 1850 and 1870, Congress granted 150,000,000 acres (an area one-and-a-half times the size of California) to western railroads. The more settlers who came west, the more valuable this land would become.

Ordinary people had also created holdings through various federal land programs. The most famous was the Homestead Act of 1862. This act

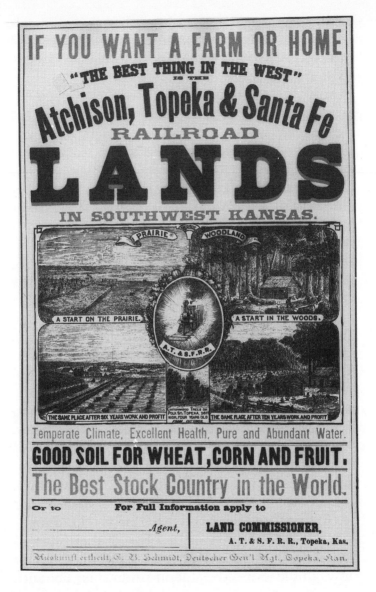

Signs advertising inexpensive land, such as this one, brought wave after wave of people to the West, all clamoring for a "place of their own."

was directed to all heads of families and all males over twenty-one. They could acquire 160 acres of land simply by living on it for five years and making some improvements.

Many settlers made good use of these acts. Others abused them. The Homestead Act required that a "dwelling" be built. Loggers, though, often put up "homes" about the size of a coffin standing on end.

People objected to these practices, but their voices often went ignored. Powerful companies spent millions of dollars protecting their interests. Much of this money was spent hiring lobbyists in Washington, D.C. These people had the job of trying to influence congressmen by discussing the issues with them.

Sometimes lobbyists used more than words. Bribes were widespread in politics. Payoffs reached even the highest levels of government. In 1873, Vice-President Schuyler Colfax and several congressmen were implicated in a scandal. They had received company stock in return for blocking an investigation of a crooked railroad construction company.

Muir did have some allies, though. Several influential Californians shared many of his views. Among them was John Strentzel, a doctor and fruit grower outside of Oakland. He and his daughter Louie ran a large ranch. A few of their mutual friends thought John Muir would enjoy getting to know Louie Strentzel. Muir didn't argue with

Schuyler Colfax, Vice-President of the United States, in 1873.

them. However, he did not get around to visiting the Strentzel ranch for several years.

In 1879, Muir helped California Senator John F. Miller develop plans to create protected parks around Yosemite. These plans would help save tracts of unspoiled land. It was land that people could visit to escape the pressures of civilization. Everyone, thought Muir, should spend some time in the wilderness. They should leave behind their worries about jobs or money. Muir believed in

California Senator John F. Miller.

what he called "the healing power of Nature." He felt everyone could benefit from it.

Unfortunately, few people agreed with him. Maintaining the wilderness didn't matter to most people. Lumberjacks didn't think about how long it would take to replace the fallen trees. Cattlemen didn't worry about the wildflowers their herds were trampling. Miners dug up the earth without caring how it would look when they were done. Their lobbyists argued against any bills that would limit their options. And so Senator Miller could not get the support he needed. His bills were voted down.

This failure disappointed Muir, but he had other things on his mind. Once he had finally gotten around to visiting the Strentzel ranch, he had gone back repeatedly. These visits to see Louie were made quietly. So it came as a surprise to many of their friends when John Muir married Louie Strentzel on April 14, 1880.

Muir spent the next ten years as a rancher. He and his wife had two daughters, and Muir introduced them to the woods and meadows. Every summer, though, he traveled for three months away from his family. He climbed mountains. He ambled through forests. It was a way of recharging his energies. The rest of the time he spent improving the family ranch.

While Muir was busy with his private life, the nation's wilderness kept shrinking. In 1880, thousands of trees were turned into almost 700 million board feet of wood. The mills ran day and night. Railroads, too, were growing quickly. In 1865 there had been only 3,272 miles of track west of the Mississippi River. By 1890 that figure would jump to 72,473 miles. The Northern Pacific Railroad, running from Minneapolis to Seattle, opened up thousands of miles of untouched land. The tracks themselves did not destroy much. But the land grants the railroad gained were as good as gold. In one later transaction, 900,000 acres (an area bigger than Rhode Island) were sold for a bit more than $5 million.

By the end of 1888, the Muirs' ranch was prospering nicely. John and Louie had all the money they needed. So they hired Muir's sister and her husband to manage the place. Now Muir could spend more time exploring, doing research, and campaigning to preserve the wilderness.

John Muir, his wife, Louie, and their two daughters.

In 1889, Muir met with Robert Underwood Johnson, editor of the well-known *Century* magazine. Johnson was a New Yorker visiting San Francisco on business. For years he had tried through letters to get Muir to resume his writing. At their first meeting, Johnson found Muir to be ". . . a farmer-looking man, black, curly hair, full long brown beard . . ." He was not the carefully groomed gentleman Johnson was. Still, the editor was very impressed.

They decided to visit Yosemite to discuss potential writing subjects. When they arrived, the subject sat there in front of them. The valley looked terrible. Trees had been recklessly cut. Meadows had been plowed. Barnyard animals were running loose wherever they pleased.

Although Yosemite was technically a state park, it was overseen rather loosely. Eight unpaid commissioners met only twice a year to consider its needs. They were subject to many political pressures. They could not protect their own positions, much less the valley itself.

It was time, said Johnson, for Yosemite to become a national park. So far the country had only one — Yellowstone — which was established in 1872. There Congress had provided for "the preservation, from injury or spoliation, of all timber, mineral deposits, natural curiosities or wonders . . ." Johnson thought that perhaps Muir could gain that same protection for Yosemite. He suggested that Muir write two articles about the valley that would publicize its unique beauty and the dangers of overdevelopment.

Muir agreed that Yosemite needed help. He wasn't sure, though, that writing articles about it would do any good. After all, Senator Miller's attempts had failed ten years earlier. Johnson was more optimistic. Times had changed, he said. He knew certain leaders who would support the plan.

So Muir went ahead and wrote the articles. They described Yosemite's beauty, but they also issued a warning: "The ground is already being gnawed and trampled into a desert, and when the region shall be stripped of its forests, the ruin will be complete."

These were powerful words, and their publication started a national debate. Many Easterners quickly approved of Muir's proposals. From their crowded cities, they saw the value of preserving land. Of course, it was also easy for them to take this view. Their own land and lives would not be affected. Westerners, on the other hand, were more worried. Putting restrictions on any land set a bad example. How many of these troublesome national parks were there going to be?

In Yosemite itself, there were many forces that didn't want it to be saved. The Yosemite Stage and Turnpike Company, which carried tourists through the valley, liked things the way they were. The owners didn't want the federal government meddling in their business. And they weren't alone. Some cattlemen and sheepherders used the land around Yosemite for their grazing herds. They didn't want that to change.

Many of these people owned California newspapers. Their friends owned them, too. So it was not surprising that these newspapers published articles against the plan. Muir himself even came under attack. One Oakland politician, John P. Irish, declared that Muir had once exploited Yosemite himself: "There he cut and logged and sawed the trees of the Valley with as willing a hand as any lumberman in the Sierras."

Muir could not stay quiet in the face of such a lie. In response, he wrote a letter to the *Oakland Tribune:* "I never cut down a single tree in the Yosemite, nor sawed a tree cut down by any other person there. Furthermore, I never held, or tried to hold any sort of the claim in the valley, or sold a foot of lumber there or elsewhere."

One unexpected ally of the park idea was the Southern Pacific Railroad. It was not known as a champion of the wilderness. Its leaders, though, were looking ahead. National parks would draw visitors to the West. Most of them would travel by train.

The first proposal that appeared before Congress was based on Muir's ideas. However, it omitted a large northern region. Muir wrote to Johnson, raising objections. The bill covered only 288 square miles. Muir had pictured a park five times that size. He wanted to save the whole region, not just a piece of it. Johnson agreed. He went to Washington and read Muir's comments before the House Committee on Public Lands.

Congress listened. However, its view remained somewhat different from Muir's. He wanted to save the wilderness for its own sake. The government was less philosophical. It looked on the land mostly for the recreational and entertainment value it gave to the public.

Still, the results were satisfying. In 1890, Yosemite National Park, an area of 1,100 square miles, was created. Two other parks, Sequoia and General Grant, were also created that year.

Of course, what the government had done, it could also undo. In February 1892, a California representative attempted to have Yosemite cut in half. He wanted the remaining land to be re-

23

opened to grazing, mining, and logging.

This plan did not go unchallenged. Muir and others took up the fight. If the park was cut in half now, surely more would be nibbled at in time. Eventually, there might be nothing left.

Fortunately, the bill was defeated. Others, however, were bound to crop up again. To help fight such efforts, the Sierra Club was created in 1892. It had 162 charter members, and John Muir became its first president. Among the club's stated purposes was engaging "the support and cooperation of the people and the government in preserving the forests and other natural features of the Sierra Nevada Mountains."

The Sierra Club, though, could not stand alone. Larger economic forces were just too powerful. The search for oil was leading wildcatters into previously barren lands. New uses for electricity were leading people to exploit rivers and waterfalls for the water power to turn turbines. Both mining and cattle-raising were becoming big business. They were run by large companies, not just cowboys or prospectors.

Muir fought on. For twenty years he led the newborn conservation movement in America. His first book, *The Mountains of California*, appeared in 1894, and others followed. Muir's vivid wilderness stories won a wide following. Not all of his allies, though, agreed with him completely. Muir was truly a preservationist. He wanted to protect the woods for their own sake. Others, called conservationists, wanted to use the earth's resources —

but wisely. Muir would have been happier letting those resources lie in peace. The real tragedy in cutting down a tree, he thought, was that the tree itself was gone.

More people might have shared Muir's views if they had visited the woods for themselves. He always encouraged people to experience the wilderness firsthand, not just read about it from a comfortable chair. Muir himself accompanied some Sierra Club members on a month-long trip to Yosemite in 1901. He made other campings in the following years.

President Theodore Roosevelt himself camped out with Muir in May 1903. They spent four days together in Yosemite. Roosevelt was an enthusiastic hunter, a former soldier at home in the wild. He was also a good talker. So was Muir. They both enjoyed themselves, and the president became a valuable friend. He later added almost 100 million acres to the nation's forest reserves.

There were still battles to come over the Grand Canyon and Arizona's Petrified Forest. Muir helped to preserve them both. His last battle was not so successful. It was a fight to save the Hetch Hetchy Valley, near Yosemite. There was a plan to dam and flood the valley, creating a new water reservoir for the growing population of San Francisco. If created, the water would forever submerge the land, even the trees, at the bottom of a man-made lake.

For years Muir and his friends tried to save the Hetch Hetchy Valley. Ultimately they lost the fight.

President Theodore Roosevelt with John Muir.

Even in defeat, though, they gained a lot of publicity and political support. The battle also contributed to the creation of the National Park Service in 1916. This new federal agency oversaw all the national parks. It would make exploiting government lands much harder to do in the future.

John Muir died in 1914, two years before the birth of the Park Service. His leadership, though, had played a large part in its creation. But neither this, nor any other individual success, was his greatest legacy.

What Muir accomplished most of all was to change the popular view of the wilderness. Traditionally, untamed forests, rocky mountains, or sun-baked deserts were looked on as places of danger. They were given little value without the roads and buildings and comforts of everyday life. John Muir had aimed to change that perception. He began his memoirs writing, "When I was a boy in Scotland I was fond of everything that was wild, and all my life I've been growing fonder and fonder of wild places and wild creatures." His greatest achievement was to plant the seed of this fondness in other people as well.

Rachel Carson.

RACHEL CARSON
Faces the Threat of a Silent Spring

The early twentieth century was an exciting time for America. Science was rapidly changing the way many people lived. They had telephones and electric lights. Airplanes were flying overhead. Radio broadcasting was attracting huge audiences. And that new-fangled contraption — the automobile — was terrorizing horses on city streets and country roads.

Traditional occupations were changing, too. In farming, for example, the tractor was replacing the horse and plow. Meanwhile, a combine-harvester enabled one person to do the work of many. Scientists had even determined the chemical makeup of dirt. It turned out to have many different ingredients. Some of them helped crops grow better. These ingredients, called fertilizers,

A combine-harvester.

could also be added to the soil to make it more productive.

There were some problems, though. Fertilizers helped weeds grow better, too. Farmers didn't like that. Weeds made harvesting harder. They competed with crops for water.

Insects were also causing more trouble. Huge fields, which were now devoted to single crops, could be a feast for a particular bug. And the bigger the field, the more bugs it attracted.

As the stakes grew, farmers needed stronger and stronger protection. Scientists experimented with chemicals to create weedkillers. Other chemical combinations produced pesticides. One of them was DDT (dichloro-diphenyl-trichloro-ethane), which had been invented in 1874. During World War II, it stopped a deadly typhus epidemic in

DDT being sprayed over forests of northern Idaho.

Italy. There was no question that DDT killed and killed fast.

In July 1945, *Reader's Digest* published a letter from a thirty-eight-year-old government nature writer. "We have all heard a lot about what DDT will soon do for us by wiping out insect pests," wrote Rachel Carson. But she also wondered "what it will do to insects that are beneficial or even essential; how it may affect waterfowl, or birds that depend on insect food; whether it may upset the whole delicate balance of nature if unwisely used."

Nobody paid much attention to this letter. Still, Rachel Carson knew what she was talking about. She was sensitive to the changes people forced on their environment. She had been born on May 27, 1907, in Springdale, a town not far from Pitts-

31

burgh, Pennsylvania. Pittsburgh was a gritty place famous for its industries — steel, oil, gas, and chemicals. Coal barges passed up the river every day. The smell of smokestacks was never very far away.

Rachel and her family had lived on a farm. They had pigs and chickens, a cow and a horse. Her father was not really a farmer, though. He had bought the land as an investment. He hoped to make money selling it off as housing lots. Unfortunately, the local economy slowed. The Carsons were lucky to sell enough land to keep themselves fed and clothed.

Rachel was often sick in her youth. Sometimes she missed school for weeks at a time. Other times her mother kept her home because some sickness was going around. There were nationwide epidemics of polio in 1916 and influenza, the flu, in 1918. The flu epidemic alone killed 500,000 people.

Rachel missed a lot of school, but she never fell behind her classmates. Her mother tutored her each day. Rachel was a determined little girl. She worked hard to keep up.

That determination eventually earned her scholarships to Pennsylvania College for Women (now Chatham College). English literature was her first major. It was an appropriate choice for someone who had always wanted to be a full-time writer. Young Rachel had been a devoted reader of *St. Nicholas*, the famous children's magazine. Each month it published a few children's stories or poems. The editors had received hundreds of entries to choose from, but eleven-year-old Rachel hadn't let that discourage her. She had submitted her writings, and in one year, the magazine published three of them.

During her sophomore year of college, though, she took a biology course that changed her perspective. Her teacher's name was Mary Skinker. Rachel had not expected much from the course, but she needed the science credit to graduate. However, she had not reckoned with Miss Skinker. This teacher strongly believed that biology was much more than a catalog of facts about nature. Biology was a key to understanding life itself.

Rachel found this approach contagious. Writing fiction could not compare with investigating natural mysteries. Much to the surprise of her other teachers, she became a science major.

This was a daring choice. Although the 1920s had opened with women getting the right to vote, they lacked many other rights. Some jobs remained closed to them, especially scientific ones. When Carson graduated from college in 1929, a woman scientist had few options. She could teach, perhaps, but she couldn't get a scientific job in industry.

The beginning of the Depression only made things worse. The stock market crash and bank failures wiped out many people's savings. Many businesses closed. One person in four was without work. Luckily, Carson had a scholarship to pursue her master's degree in marine zoology at Johns Hopkins University in Baltimore. She did not find permanent work in her field until 1935.

That job was at the United States Bureau of Fisheries. The head of the Division of Scientific Inquiry, Elmer Higgins, needed a writer to work on a weekly radio program. He took a chance on Rachel Carson, and she didn't disappoint him. One job led to another. By 1945, when she wrote the letter to *Reader's Digest*, she had spent ten years working for the United States Fish and Wildlife Service.

All of her jobs had involved writing and editing. Many of them had concerned waterways and the sea. For someone raised in western Pennsylvania, Carson had an unusual love for the sea. She loved to write about it, too. In 1937, her first prominent articles about the sea had appeared in *The Atlantic* magazine. Four years later, her first book, *Under the Sea-Wind*, was published. It was an introduction to life in the ocean — for the birds on the surface and the fish beneath it. The book drew positive reviews. Unfortunately, it was mostly overlooked as the country entered World War II.

The Sea Around Us, her second book, was published in 1950. Many people had written about the sea before, but few had Carson's special viewpoint. She tried to share the perspective of the sea creatures. Before this, most science books were dull. Many nature books were unscientific. Carson managed to combine the best aspects of each. She wrote about the facts of nature without losing sight of its beauty.

The book became a national best-seller. In just

a few months it sold over 100,000 copies. Eventually, it was translated into many languages around the world.

The success of *The Sea Around Us* came at a time when the government's mood was changing. Dwight D. Eisenhower had just been elected president. He was the first Republican president in twenty years. His administration wished to relax the existing conservation policies. It wanted to open the forests and mountains, and rivers and lakes to more development.

Rachel Carson was now editor-in-chief of all the Fish and Wildlife Service's publications. However, the new government policies were edging her department in directions that made her uncomfortable. The income from her books had made her financially independent, so she resigned from government service. Afterward she wrote to the *Washington Post*, objecting to the government's change in mood. Her letter stated that "... The real wealth of the Nation lies in the resources of the earth — soil, water, forests, minerals, and wildlife." Using them properly required more care than the government seemed to be interested in.

At the time, not many people shared her view. Developing natural resources was just another part of modern life. National parks and wildlife sanctuaries were acceptable, of course — as long as they didn't get in the way. People had spent thousands of years learning how to control nature. Now it would put that control to good use.

Some of this control, though, was not as complete as people might have wished. The heralded weedkillers and pesticides were not just killing weeds and insect pests. They were landing on plants and animals, contaminating the food chain.

The food chain is a basic element of nature. Tiny plants and animals are eaten by small plants and animals. Small plants and animals are eaten by medium-sized plants and animals. Medium-sized plants and animals are eaten by large plants and animals. These large plants and animals are either eaten by other large plants and animals or are left alone to do as they please.

Rachel Carson knew all about food chains. She had written about them in her latest book, *The Edge of the Sea*. Appropriately, she had written much of it at her new summer house in Maine. The house was her special delight. She had it built close to a cliff facing Boothbay Harbor. Its many windows looked out at the tall trees and rocky beach.

Although Carson had never married, she had also never lived alone. Her mother, now in her eighties, had lived with her since the Depression. Carson had also helped raise two nieces after the death of her older sister. One of those nieces had a son, Roger. His great-aunt Rachel took a great interest in the baby boy. She especially liked to take him for walks along the beach. She marveled at the innocent joy Roger showed in his meetings with nature. She wrote of these experiences for a magazine. Later, they were published as a book, *The Sense of Wonder*.

When Roger's mother unexpectedly died of pneumonia in 1957, he went to live with his great-aunt Rachel. Taking charge of a small boy, though, was a lot of responsibility. Her mother, now eighty-nine, was also requiring more attention.

In the midst of these changes, Carson received a letter from a friend, Olga Huckins. Mrs. Huckins and her husband lived in Duxbury, Massachusetts. Olga wrote that the state had recently sprayed DDT in the area to kill mosquitoes. The spraying, however, had immediately killed many birds on her land. Others had died in the days that followed.

The state government had assured Mrs. Huckins that the spray was harmless to people. She remained unconvinced. And so now she was writing to Rachel. Did Rachel know anyone who could do something about this?

The letter was definitely troubling. Carson and a few others had already spoken out publicly against DDT. Nobody had listened. Since then, DDT and similar chemicals had become increasingly popular. They seemed to be miracle workers — saving farmers time, energy, and money.

Mosquitoes were not sprayed because they threatened crops. They were sprayed because they bit people, and sometimes these bites were more than itchy. They carried diseases, too. Spraying DDT effectively kept the mosquito population down. Olga Huckins was not the only one who had noticed the connection between DDT spraying and dead birds, but she was the only one who had written Rachel Carson about it.

Dichloro-diphenyl-trichloro-ethane, otherwise known as DDT.

Those dead birds symbolized a danger that needed to be publicized. But Carson did not expect to lead the charge herself. She had different book projects in mind. But when other writers whom she knew passed on the subject, she was unwilling to put it aside. She wrote to her editor, William Shawn, at *The New Yorker* magazine. She mentioned the idea of writing "an article that would also serve as a chapter of a book on this subject, then also perhaps an introduction and some general editorial work . . ."

Carson began her research knowing the issue went beyond the dangers of pesticides. She wanted to draw attention to the reckless treatment people gave the natural world. It soon became clear that this "chapter" would become at least a brief book. She hoped to have a finished manuscript in a few months. The working title was *The Control of Nature.*

New articles drew her notice. Roy Barker of the Illinois Natural History Survey had followed the trail of DDT through several carriers. Apparently when an elm tree was sprayed with DDT, many leaves fell to the ground. These leaves, still coated with DDT, were eaten by earthworms. If the earthworms ate too much DDT, they died at once. If not, they passed along whatever DDT they had absorbed to their offspring or to any birds that ate them. Since DDT remained poisonous for years, the young earthworms or hungry birds carried it along. Sooner or later, some animal ate too many contaminated earthworms or too many contaminated birds — and died.

From other scientists Carson learned that DDT was spreading everywhere. It had been found in birds, fish, and small mammals all over the country. Traces had even been discovered near the North and South Poles. The more she worked, the more she needed to learn. This book was going to take longer than she had thought.

In June 1959, *Reader's Digest* published an article by Robert S. Strother called "Backfire in the War Against Insects." It noted that pesticides that killed pests also killed the pests' natural enemies — birds, spiders, etc. However, the few insect pests that somehow survived the pesticides now found their natural enemies were gone. Without those enemies, the pests multiplied again quickly.

Spraying the new pesticides also led to unexpected casualties. Even a hint of DDT could affect the birthrate of fish and birds. Sometimes, too, the wrong insects were eliminated. Without these helpful insects, new problems arose.

People might have assumed that the government was watching over the use of such powerful chemicals. Carson learned otherwise. The government was exercising very little control. In fact, government agencies worked closely with the chemical industry through research and grants.

Carson was going to expose this cozy relationship, a step she knew would cause trouble. As she wrote to her friend and former boss Clarence Cottam, "the whole thing is so explosive, and the pressures on the other side so powerful and enormous, that I feel it far wiser to keep my own counsel insofar as I can until I am ready to launch my attack as a whole."

The hurdles she faced were not only professional. Her mother had died in December of 1958. It was a hard parting. They had lived together almost all of Rachel's life. Then in 1960, Carson learned she had cancer. In April she underwent surgery. Her prospects were not good. She might live one more year — or five. Either way, she had no time to feel sorry for herself. There was too much important work to do.

One problem Carson wrestled with was how to write about scientific things for the average reader. DDT was part of a family of pesticides called chlorinated hydrocarbons. That was certainly a mouthful — more than most people would be willing to swallow. How was she going to hold their interest? How was she going to make them understand the important connection between pollution and public health?

The words came slowly. She wrote:

These sprays, dusts, and aerosols . . . have the power to kill every insect, the "good" and the "bad," to still the song of birds and the leaping of fish in the streams, to coat the leaves with a deadly film, and to linger on in the soil — all this though the intended target may be only a few weeds or insects. Can anyone believe it is possible to lay down such a barrage of poisons on the surface of the earth without making it unfit for all life?

Though she loved writing, it had always been hard work. Her worsening health made the struggle even greater. She still enjoyed the summers in Maine. But now she tired easily. In the fall, she began radiation treatments. As her resistance weakened, she caught the flu and an intestinal virus. Then a winter infection in her knees and ankles kept her in bed for weeks.

After another slow year, she began showing the manuscript to a few people. Professional and personal friends warned her that the chemical industry would return her attack. Clarence Cottam wrote her in early 1962 that "you are going to be subjected to ridicule and condemnation by a few."

Carson was unhappy about this, but the prospect did not stop her. When she began her book in 1958, the chemical industry had sold almost

$200,000,000 worth of pesticides. In the four years since then, that annual amount had more than doubled. Someone had to do something about it.

As Carson wrote to a friend, "The beauty of the living world I was trying to save has always been uppermost in my mind — that, and anger at the senseless, brutish things that were being done."

The first excerpt from her book, called *Silent Spring*, appeared on June 16, 1962, in *The New Yorker* magazine. (Two more parts followed.) She began it with a fable, a story of an imaginary farming town. All was well there until "a strange blight crept over the area . . ." Not long after that, a day came when no birds sang. Cattle and sheep died. What had caused this silent spring? That was what the rest of the book was about.

Reaction came swiftly. The next month a *New York Times* article was headlined "*Silent Spring* Is Now Noisy Summer." Noisy was right. *Silent Spring* was news, and almost everyone had an opinion about it. Dozens of newspaper editorials and columns were favorable. Some were not. Among the national journals, *Time* magazine in particular thought Carson was worrying too much.

The excerpts drew attention from other quarters, too. As her friends had predicted, *Silent Spring* was not a book the chemical industry could ignore. Carson herself was too famous, and the financial stakes too high, to let her claims pass unchallenged.

The counterattack took many forms. The Vel-

Rachel Carson with a copy of her book, Silent Spring.

sicol Chemical Corporation of Chicago immediately wrote to Carson's publisher, Houghton Mifflin, advising them to halt publication because the book criticized two chemicals Velsicol manufactured. Their letter warned that the book's false claims could hobble the chemical industry. The nation's food supply would suffer.

To be fair and to protect itself, Houghton Mifflin investigated Velsicol's objections. Its report revealed no grounds for concern. Publication continued as planned.

Chemical companies searched every page, looking for errors. The National Agricultural Chemicals Association budgeted $250,000 for a booklet refuting Carson's facts. Various organizations copied and distributed critical reviews of and articles about *Silent Spring*. Over and over they trumpeted the same themes: Pesticides were good. Pesticides were necessary. Pesticides were the last defense against hunger and disease.

Rachel Carson knew the chemical industry would not like her book. But she was surprised at the negative reaction among government agencies. The problem there, however, was embarrassment. Having encouraged pesticide development, government officials were feeling defensive. It was easier to criticize Rachel Carson than to admit their mistake.

At the highest level, however, the reaction was different. Both President John F. Kennedy and Secretary of Agriculture Orville Freeman took the book quite seriously. They ordered a review of Carson's claims from the President's Scientific Advisory Committee (PSAC).

Carson herself tried to stay clear of the attacks. Her determination had not wavered. Her book had been necessary. It was painful, though, that the criticisms were not limited to the book itself. Some were directed at her, saying that Carson was a dreamer. She was too sentimental. She was no scientist, just another nature fanatic.

None of these comments hurt the book financially. *Silent Spring* was published on September 27, 1962. Advance sales were 40,000. By December, 100,000 copies had been sold.

The late fall was crowded with many *Silent Spring* events. There were luncheons, receptions, and autographing parties in various cities. In a speech to the Women's National Press Club on December 5, Carson answered some of her critics:

One obvious way to try to weaken a cause is to discredit the person who champions it. So the masters of invective and insinuation have been busy: I am a bird lover — a cat lover — a fish lover — a priestess of nature . . .

Anyone who has really read the book knows that I criticize the modern chemical method not because it controls harmful insects but because it controls them badly and ineffectively and creates many dangerous side effects in doing so.

Appearing before a Senate Government Operations subcommittee, Rachel Carson called for strict control of aerial pesticide spraying.

One prominent critic of *Silent Spring* had been Robert H. White-Stevens. He worked for the American Cyanamid Company. On April 3, 1963, he and Rachel Carson, along with several high government representatives, appeared on a CBS television program, "The Silent Spring of Rachel Carson."

It had been difficult for Carson to agree to participate. Her worsening health was making it harder to keep up public appearances. Walking was often difficult. Sometimes her eyesight failed her. Still, she summoned the strength to appear.

The program explored both sides of the issues. Mr. White-Stevens made the major attack on *Silent Spring*: "If man were to faithfully follow the teachings of Miss Carson," he said, "we would return to the Dark Ages, and the insects and vermin would once again inherit the earth." Later, he added, "Miss Carson maintains that the balance of nature is a major force in the survival of man; whereas the modern scientist believes that man is steadily controlling nature . . ."

Rachel Carson made a careful reply. Some people might think, she said, that "the balance of nature is something that was repealed as soon as man came on the scene. You might just as well assume that you could repeal the law of gravity. The balance of nature is built of a series of interrelationships between living things, and between living things and their environment. This doesn't mean that we must not attempt to tilt the balance of nature in our favor; but when we do make this attempt we must know what we're doing. We must know the consequences."

A few weeks later, on May 15, the PSAC's report was released. It looked carefully at both the advantages and drawbacks of pesticides. Generally, the report shared Rachel Carson's conclusions. The use of pesticides needed greater control. The report ended by saying that ". . . until the publication of *Silent Spring* by Rachel Carson, people were generally unaware of the toxicity of pesticides. The Government should present this information to the public in a way that will make it aware of the dangers while recognizing the value of pesticides."

This had been Carson's aim all along. She had not called for a ban on all pesticides. She did want DDT banned because of the way it moved poisonously through the environment. Other pesticides should simply be used with more concern for the larger ecological picture.

Many publications that previously had been critical of *Silent Spring* approved of the PSAC report. Others, including *Time*, changed their earlier objections. Many states passed bills to oversee the distribution and use of pesticides. In the past, the government needed to show a chemical was dangerous to have it removed from the market. But in 1964, Congress changed federal law: chemical companies would now have to prove a product was safe before it could be sold.

The *Silent Spring* debate was not limited to the United States. The book was translated into many languages. All over the world, Carson's words fostered a reexamination of the careless use of chemicals.

Rachel Carson did not live to see all of these things happen. In 1963, she had a heart attack. It further drained her strength and energy. In her last summer in Maine, she could no longer walk along the shore. But she was content to watch from her deck, close to the sights and sounds of the sea.

In the winter of 1964 she received many honors and awards. She enjoyed them in her fashion, but she remained surprised that she was receiving so much attention.

When Rachel died on April 14, her friends and her countless readers mourned her passing. In the

U.S. Senate, Senator Abraham Ribicoff of Connecticut spoke of "this gentle lady who aroused people everywhere to be concerned with one of the most significant problems of mid-twentieth century life — man's contamination of his environment."

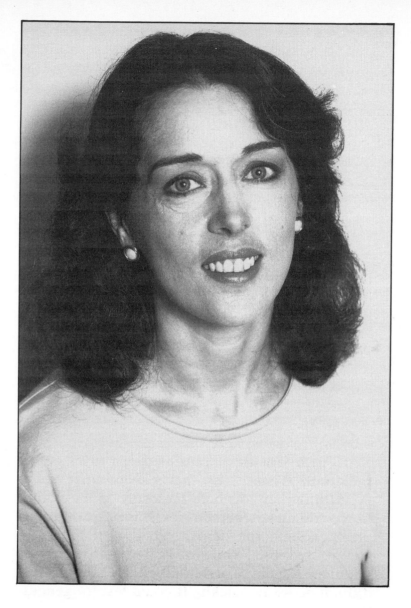

Lois Gibbs.

LOIS GIBBS
and the Unearthing of Love Canal

On August 6, 1945, the United States dropped an atomic bomb on the Japanese city of Hiroshima. The enormous destruction helped end World War II. But the use of an atomic bomb meant more than just greater explosive power. Other bombs, regardless of their power, had no aftereffects. Once the bombs had exploded, the damage was done.

Atomic bombs were different. Their explosion sent out a stream of poisonous particles called radiation. These tiny particles contaminated everything they touched. Exposure to this radiation could make a person sick. If the exposure was great enough, the person would die. Someone could get exposed while eating or breathing or just sitting in a chair. Worst of all, this contamination did not go away quickly. It could last for generations.

The world's first atomic bomb was tested near Alamogordo, New Mexico, on July 16, 1945.

Radiation was so small and light that the wind could carry it great distances. It could also travel in water. A bomb set off in one place could contaminate an area hundreds of miles away. The poisonous radiation could be passed from one source to another. If a cow ate radioactive grass, its milk would be radioactive, too. Despite these facts, the United States continued to test new bombs. Other countries did the same.

The first nuclear test ban treaty was finally signed in 1963 by the United States, the Soviet Union, and Great Britain. Almost a hundred other countries also signed it. They agreed to no longer set off atomic bombs in the atmosphere, the ocean, or in space. (Bombs could still be set off underground.) This agreement sharply cut the amount of radiation contaminating the earth.

Radiation was a very dramatic example of hazardous waste. People, though, had been handling materials carelessly or misusing them for thousands of years. Ancient Romans made pots, cups, and plates with lead, unaware that the soft metal was poisonous. The lead rubbed off into the food and drink, poisoning some of them. More recently, goldsmiths and hatters (people who made hats) used mercury in their work. The mercury was absorbed through their skin. Sometimes it affected their brains. These tragic effects led to the expression "mad as a hatter."

Lois Conn was twelve years old in 1963, the year of the test ban treaty. If she knew anything about mad hatters, it was only that one was a character in *Alice in Wonderland*. Lois was living in Grand Island, New York, not far from Buffalo. Her father was a bricklayer. Her mother took care of the family. It was a large family — Lois was the third of six boys and girls.

Being in the middle of six children was a good place to develop self-reliance. When Lois wanted seconds at dinner, she had to move fast. Still, she was a shy child. She had a few friends, but she did most things with her brothers and sisters.

Lois grew up in the 1960s, a time of uneasiness about the environment. It wasn't just radiation that worried people. The fumes from cars and trucks were choking cities. Fish disappeared from many polluted rivers. Factories spewed forth unhealthy gases and smoke.

None of this was a big problem in Grand Island, though. There Lois mostly kept to herself. She wasn't active in sports or other school organizations. Her main hobby was sewing. She made many curtains and bedspreads. It was painstaking work, but Lois liked it. Sewing brought out her creative side.

After she graduated from high school in 1969, she went off to work in Buffalo. She didn't have any special career plans. Her first job was as a department store salesclerk. Later she became a nurse's aide in a nursing home. It was satisfying to help older people who weren't always able to help themselves.

While she worked, environmental issues were getting more publicity. Many people feared that the earth might soon choke to death on its own waste products. On April 21, 1970, the first Earth Day was celebrated. This was a widespread demonstration against the pollution that threatened the earth. The next December, Congress created the Environmental Protection Agency (EPA). The EPA was supposed to be the nation's ecological watchdog. One of its goals was to keep pollution from overpowering the country's cities.

One such city was Niagara Falls, New York. It is most famous for its falls, which were formed by a retreating glacier 10,000 years ago. The city itself was founded as a trading outpost in the 1680s.

The plentiful water power later drew industry to the spot. Over time, Niagara Falls grew into a small industrial city. In 1972, over 70,000 people lived there.

One of them was Lois Gibbs. The former Lois Conn was twenty-one years old now — and married. Her husband was Harry Gibbs, a chemical worker. They had a son, Michael, who was just a few months old. The Gibbses had just bought their first home, a three-bedroom bungalow on 101st Street. As Lois Gibbs later wrote: "It was a lovely neighborhood in a quiet residential area, with lots of trees and lots of children outside playing. It seemed just the place for our family."

This neighborhood was known as the Love Canal section of the city. It was named for William T. Love, a local nineteenth-century businessman. In 1892, he had put together a hydroelectric power plan that included building a seven-mile-long canal connecting the upper and lower Niagara River. Unfortunately, the project lost its financial support long before the canal was finished. Love eventually abandoned it and went on to other things.

The unfinished canal remained behind. It was a mile-long hole, ten to forty feet deep and forty-five feet wide. The canal had been filled in long before the Gibbses had bought their house. The area, though, had kept the name.

While Harry Gibbs went off to work each day, Lois Gibbs stayed home. She cooked and cleaned and took care of the children. In 1975, the Gibbses

An aerial view of the Love Canal neighborhood. The houses near the bottom of the picture were abandoned soon after discovery of the contamination.

had a daughter, Melissa. She and Michael kept their mother very busy.

The mid 1970s were wet years for Niagara Falls. There was a lot more rain and snow than usual. For the Gibbses, the extra rain and snow did not seem like a big problem. But when the ground could not absorb any more water, things began to happen. In October 1974, a nearby backyard fiberglass swimming pool was pushed right out of the ground. The ground water that had pushed it also turned out to be polluted. It ate into the wooden fence posts and withered the bushes.

This was strange, but no stranger than other problems that already existed in the neighborhood. Even before the flooding, many basements were filled with terrible odors. Some residents had lived for years with mysterious rashes or coughs that never went away.

The neighbors didn't really talk about their troubles. Everyone knew Niagara Falls had many chemical plants. Nobody liked the chemical smells, which often seemed to reach right into a house. But people were used to them. And the jobs the chemical companies provided were important to the community.

Traditionally, the biggest concern in waste disposal had been keeping it from attracting flies. This was certainly important when filling a dump with garbage. But modern landfills were collecting other things besides decomposed food. Leftover chemicals from industrial processes were often thrown out with little more care than a banana peel. Most of them ended up as sludge, a mixture of solids and liquids that looked like watery mud. This untreated sludge was often buried in barrels or just emptied into open, unlined pits.

In 1976, Congress finally created legislation acknowledging the dangers of hazardous waste. The Resource Conservation and Recovery Act (RCRA) required that hazardous waste be monitored from its creation onward. However, companies were expected to do their own monitoring. This certainly left room for abuse, but at least it was a start.

The RCRA was not designed, though, to do anything about chemicals already in the ground. Some of these chemicals were the subject of a June 1978 story about Love Canal that appeared in the *Niagara Gazette*. It was part of a series written by Michael Brown. The story explained that traces of industrial chemicals had been found in the 97th–99th Streets area. Brown reported that many residents suffered from health problems these chemicals could have caused.

Lois Gibbs read the story, but she wasn't concerned for her family at first. Their house, after all, didn't border the former canal. It was several blocks away.

Then she realized something. The 99th Street School, where Michael went to kindergarten, sat right on top of the former canal. How safe could this school be? Michael already had some health problems. He was taking medication for seizures. And his white blood cell count was lower than normal (making him more vulnerable to infection). Were these chemicals in the ground causing his troubles or at least making them worse?

The Gibbses tried to get Michael transferred to another school. But school officials questioned the move. They felt Mrs. Gibbs worried too much. The superintendent needed more proof to justify a transfer. He wanted letters from two doctors stating that Michael should be moved for medical reasons.

Lois Gibbs got those letters right away — from Michael's pediatrician and the family doctor. But the superintendent still was not satisfied. The let-

Government officials outside the 99th Street Elementary School.

ters, he said, were based on the idea that the area was contaminated. If this was true, then all the children should be transferred. But the superintendent didn't believe this. The school was only about twenty years old. It was in perfectly good condition. Therefore, he denied her request.

In most matters, Lois Gibbs would never have dreamed of doubting a superintendent of schools. But she doubted now. The superintendent had not really explained anything to her. He had said nothing reassuring. She could not let his decision go unchallenged.

Gibbs was still a shy person, but she was also stubborn. Michael's health was at stake. The health of the other schoolchildren was in danger, too. She had to try something. All she could think of, though, was starting a petition to close the school. If enough people signed it, maybe the board of education would act.

Getting signatures on a petition meant going door-to-door. Just the idea of it made Lois Gibbs nervous. She had never even sold Girl Scout cookies. What would people say to her when she appeared uninvited on their doorstep? They might be rude. They might think she was crazy.

Still, she had to try. She began at a house on the street spotlighted in the newspaper articles. But she barely got started. She was too nervous. She retreated home in fear after knocking on just one door — and nobody was home.

The next day she tried again, this time on her own street. That went better. These were her neighbors. She baby-sat for some of their children. Each day she went out, she grew a little more confident.

At some houses she often spent twenty minutes or more discussing the situation. Among other things, she shared the story of the canal's later history. For many years after William Love had abandoned it, the canal had just sat there. Some of it had filled up with water. People used it for swimming in the summer and ice-skating in the winter.

In the 1940s, the land was sold to the Hooker

Chemical Company. Hooker's products ranged from pesticides to lye (an ingredient in some kinds of soap). Naturally, making these products generated waste, often in the form of oily fluids and bubbling sludge. Most of them were toxic.

From the mid 1940s until 1953, Hooker used the giant hole as a chemical disposal site. More than 20,000 tons of waste were buried in the former canal. They were dumped in large metal barrels. The United States Army and other federal agencies may have dumped waste there, too.

In 1953, Hooker sold the Love Canal land to the local board of education for one dollar. It seemed like a bargain. However, the property deed mentioned that the land contained "waste products from the manufacture of chemicals." So the token price was more than just a generous gift. The sale was also supposed to shield Hooker from any problems the buried wastes might later create. However, nobody from the company explained (and no one from the board really asked them) what these future problems might be.

The board of education was just happy to get the free land. Even when the architect raised questions about the chemicals in the ground, they were not overly concerned. The architect wasn't sure what the chemicals in the ground might do to the foundation. The board agreed to move the school a few yards. They never seriously reconsidered building it somewhere else.

Few residents of the Love Canal area knew these facts. Everyone, though, had heard of Hooker

Chemical Company. It had several plants in and around Niagara Falls, as well as in other places. In 1978, the company had net sales of $1.7 billion. It employed a lot of people from Niagara Falls, including some who lived in the neighborhood. These people were reluctant to complain. Couldn't they just ignore the problem and hope it would go away by itself?

Lois Gibbs didn't think so. The newspaper articles had prompted the New York State Department of Health to arrange a public meeting. Gibbs was one of the seventy-five people who attended. One man reported that the ground in his backyard had burned his baby daughter's bare feet. How could this happen? A woman stated that her dog had burned his nose while sniffing the ground.

The health department representatives promised to investigate. They already planned to test the houses and property bordering the former canal for traces of dangerous chemicals. Residents of those houses were also being asked to take blood tests. Meanwhile the state would install a filtering system around the canal border. This system would supposedly eliminate the chemical seepage.

Lois Gibbs was not satisfied. She was glad the state was starting a surface cleanup, but what about underground contamination? And what about the 99th Street school? Was it safe or not?

The representatives didn't have answers for these questions. They tried to be reassuring. On the one hand, they told everyone not to worry. On the other, they advised Love Canal residents not to eat anything from their gardens.

Lois Gibbs wasn't worried about her vegetables. But she was worried. A small group, including herself, her brother-in-law, and some neighbors, met with their state representatives to discuss the situation. They wrote to their senators and talked to a lawyer. Maybe they were going to have to sue somebody.

Other government meetings were held. They took place in Niagara Falls and the state capital, Albany, 300 miles away. Gibbs carpooled to an important Albany meeting on August 2. There she heard what Commissioner Robert Whalen of the State Department of Health had to report.

The commissioner didn't mince words. "A review of all the available evidence respecting the Love Canal Chemical Waste Landfill has convinced me of a great and immediate peril to the health of the general public residing at or near the site." He then made several announcements. The 99th Street School would be closed for the present. Pregnant women and children under the age of two should leave the southern edge of the canal area. The remaining residents should avoid going into their basements as much as possible.

These statements exploded over the Love Canal community. A meeting was hastily set up for the next day. Many questions remained unanswered. Why were only pregnant women at risk? What about women who wanted to become pregnant? What made two years old the cutoff? Why only the

Students protesting the government's reluctance to relocate Love Canal residents.

southern edge? And how were people supposed to just *leave*? Were families supposed to split up? Where was everyone going to stay?

As one of the few residents who had heard Commissioner Whalen in person, Gibbs addressed the group. It was a hard moment for her. "I had never spoken to a group in my whole life," she wrote afterwards. "In high school, if I had to do a book report in front of the class, I would cut the class."

Gibbs told the crowd what she knew, but the news was not encouraging. The next day another meeting was held. Here residents created the Love Canal Homeowners Association. The association boundaries included 789 single homes and 250 rental units. The association set four goals. The first was to move from the area all residents who wanted to be relocated. The second was to somehow stabilize property values. The third was to get the canal fixed. And the fourth was to get the area's air, water, and soil tested.

In a brief vote, Lois Gibbs was elected the association's first president. She could hardly believe it. She had met her original goal — getting the school closed. Now she had become the president of an organization representing hundreds of families. This meant she would be meeting with the governor or other important people. These people had all gone to college. She had not. They were well-spoken, well-dressed, and used to getting their way.

Gibbs was used to none of these things. But she was too busy to be intimidated. Reporters were calling with questions. There were interviews on television. A few days later she was invited to a meeting in Washington at the White House. It was exciting to go, but she had to borrow the money for the plane ticket.

There were a thousand things to organize. She accepted the challenge. Running a family took organization. This was just a different kind. She was going to need patience and persistence. Well, she needed those things raising her children and doing her intricate sewing, too.

She would not have much room to make mistakes. People were angry — at the city, at the state, and at the Hooker Chemical Company. Spokesmen for Hooker, however, maintained that the company had always acted responsibly. The clay canal bed had made a proper disposal site in its time. And before Hooker had sold the land, the top of the canal had also been covered with clay. The company maintained that this clay container, if left undisturbed, would have safely held the chemicals forever.

Clearly, the surface had been disturbed a lot. The school, roads, and sewers had broken the seal many times. For twenty years the chemicals slowly had been seeping into the surrounding ground. The recent heavy rain and snow simply had sped up the process.

A few days later, the state agreed to move families whose homes touched the canal site. They would be relocated temporarily in motels at state

Abandoned houses in the Love Canal neighborhood became a familiar sight.

expense. And the state would also buy their homes at fair market value.

The federal government was also about to declare Love Canal a disaster area. This would make federal funds available for a cleanup. The total costs of a cleanup and relocation were estimated at $22 million.

This was good news. But to Lois Gibbs and the Love Canal Homeowners Association, it was only the beginning. The state was suggesting that the crisis was now under control. But what about the houses a few more yards away? Did the chemicals know they weren't supposed to cross a street or seep under a backyard fence? Was it possible that underground streams could have carried the contamination even farther?

67

These were uncomfortable questions. City officials shied away from answering them. They were concerned that the bad publicity could affect the tourist trade — an important part of the area's economy. The state, too, sent confusing signals. Various state agencies, playing musical chairs with the environmental tests, seemed disorganized and inefficient. Eventually, though, the evacuation was enlarged to include another ring of homes.

Such confusion helps explain why so few remaining residents just picked up and moved. They could not afford to pay house mortgage payments and the rent somewhere else. They knew there were health risks in staying. But they were sure the state government was always just about to bail them out. Nobody wanted to gamble that the day *after* the bank repossessed their house, the government would agree to buy it. So they hung on, hoping the state would act soon.

But the state wasn't about to rescue them, at least not without a push.

As the months passed, Lois Gibbs grew into her new position. It was an uncomfortable fit at first. Her life once had been neat and orderly. Her only visitors had been family and a few friends. Now there were daily meetings and problems to solve. She had to learn to use her words carefully, to make a point quickly. It seemed as if neighbors, politicians, and reporters were constantly underfoot.

The job itself took up almost all her time, and she was still a volunteer. Nobody working for the

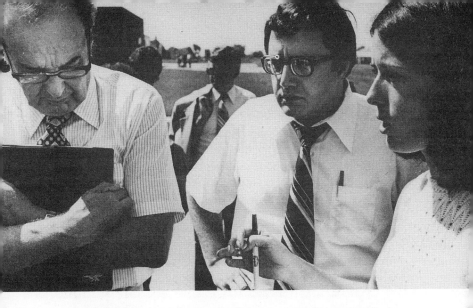

Lois Gibbs tours the Love Canal area with government officials.

association was paid. The money raised from members' dues, bake sales, and raffles went to pay expenses.

Over time she also became more politically aware. Going to the newspapers or television stations was her most powerful weapon. "I never thought government worked like that," she wrote later. "I thought that if you had a complaint, you went to the right person in the government, and if there was a way to solve the problem or alleviate it, that they would be glad to do it. I was to learn differently."

Her role required a certain amount of juggling. She saw to the concerns of residents. She kept up with the needs of the media. She made speeches

69

and appeared on television talk shows. She even made her way through the maze of government bureaucracies. Sometimes her actions outraged officials, who wished she would just go away. But she didn't.

At the same time, her responsibilities changed her personal life. She could barely keep track of which day it was. It was exciting to speak before committees in Washington. It was hard, though, to be away from her husband and children. Her whole life had turned upside down.

That December of 1978, the pressure increased. Traces of the chemical dioxin were discovered in the area. Dioxin is so toxic that its safety limits are measured in parts per trillion. Eventually, traces of over 400 chemicals were found in the Love Canal area. Some of them were measured in levels thousands of times greater than was considered safe.

And Love Canal was not alone. In late 1978, an EPA survey identified 32,000 places nationwide where hazardous waste had been improperly deposited. Treating them properly was going to involve recycling programs, incineration, and filtering systems. Even so, the cleanup would take many years.

In February 1979, New York State offered to move pregnant women and children under the age of two from a much wider area than at first indicated. Again, a cry went up over these choices. Weren't men at risk, too? What about teenagers or toddlers? How was the state making such distinctions?

This tug-of-war between state agencies and the Love Canal Homeowners Association continued for months to come. The residents wrote letters and made phone calls. They even held parades to keep their plight in the public eye. At one point, Gibbs and some other association members transported two fake coffins to Albany — one for an adult and one for a child. They intended to deliver them to the governor. The message was clear: People were still dying because of Love Canal. What was the state going to do about it?

For Lois Gibbs, the days when her biggest problem was picking out wallpaper seemed like a distant memory. It wasn't just that she was doing so many things at once. She, too, was a victim of Love Canal. She had to deal with her own emotions as well. Her own family had finally been evacuated to a nearby motel. The four of them were crammed into one room. The state was paying their bill, and hundreds of others', too. Something had to change.

It did, finally, but not for another year. On May 21, 1980, President Jimmy Carter declared a health emergency in the Love Canal area. This declaration came after an EPA report was released. It stated that residents had a higher chance of getting cancer, bearing children with birth defects, and other medical problems.

That summer the federal government and New York State worked out a loan and grant agreement allowing the state to buy all the Love Canal area homes. In October, President Jimmy Carter signed a bill authorizing the permanent evacuation of all families from Love Canal. By February 1981, 400 families had been moved from Love Canal. The issue of blame was still unsettled, but there was more than enough blame for the Niagara Falls Board of Education, the city, and the state to share.

As for the Hooker Chemical Company, it had spent more than $250,000 on newspaper ads explaining its position. Thousands of pamphlets were sent out to newspapers and influential people to give Hooker's side of the story. Still, in 1983, the company paid millions of dollars to residents in an out-of-court settlement. Government lawsuits concerning the cleanup and relocation costs were later dropped when the company agreed to reimburse the government for these expenses.

The Love Canal Homeowners Association's victory was bittersweet. The delays in moving people had caused further hardships and health hazards. All the confusion, the danger, and the terrible waiting took its toll. Some marriages broke up, Lois Gibbs's among them. She could not return to the life she had known before. She was no longer the same person.

After her divorce, she moved to the Washington, D.C., area with her two children. There she created the Citizen's Clearinghouse for Hazardous Waste to advise others who are threatened by hazardous waste problems and to lobby Congress on environmental issues. She serves as the organization's executive director. She has since remarried and has two more young sons.

In 1990, twelve years after Lois Gibbs first went door-to-door, New York State offered some of the Love Canal homes for sale. The state insisted that they are now safe for inhabitation. Maybe they are. The experience of Lois Gibbs, though, suggests that there are some things nobody should take for granted.

Chico Mendes.

CHICO MENDES
and the Preservation of the Amazon Rain Forest

The Amazon River basin covers over 3.6 million square miles. This area, most of it in Brazil, is almost as big as the continental United States. Two-thirds of it is covered by rain forest. It is the largest area of continuous forest in the world.

The first Europeans to travel the 4,000-mile-long Amazon River were the Spanish conquistadors. A group of them got lost on the Amazon in 1541 while searching for the legendary city of El Dorado. They killed many of the Indians they met. When their supplies ran out, they ate their belts and the soles of their shoes. Eight months and 2,400 miles later, they finally reached the Atlantic Ocean.

No one ever found El Dorado. But in the 1800s, Brazilian pioneers found wealth in the rain forest's woods — chicle (for chewing gum) and Brazil

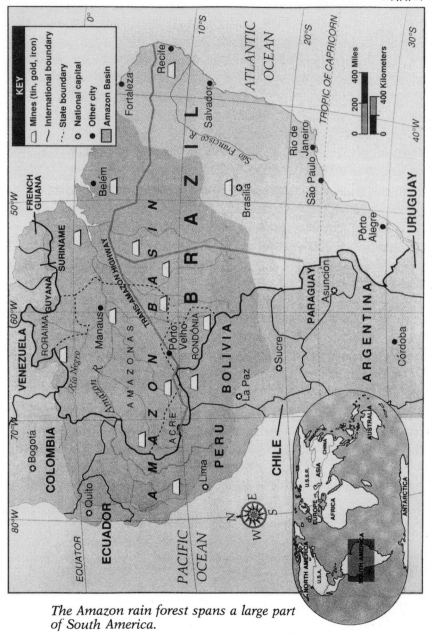

The Amazon rain forest spans a large part
of South America.

nuts. Another resource came from the tree the Indians called "the wood that weeps." This tree grows one hundred feet tall. When the trunk is cut, it bleeds a white sticky liquid called latex. When latex is processed, it repels water, insulates against electricity, and bounces. These properties make latex, or rubber, a very useful thing.

Two groups of people live in and near the rain forest — those who make their living from the rain forest, and those who make their living in spite of it. Francisco Alves Mendes Filho, known to everyone as Chico Mendes, was proud to be in the first group. He was a rubber tapper, a *seringueiro*.

As a boy, Chico Mendes had learned to harvest latex from the rubber tree. He had seventeen brothers and sisters (only six lived to adulthood). Almost everything they ate or wore or used came from the land around them. There were no schools for tapper children then. Young Chico's father taught him to read. He also taught him the names and uses of the different trees.

At nine, Chico was helping his father in his work. By the time he was eleven, he was harvesting full time. Every day he was up before dawn. He carried a homemade kerosene lamp to help him see in the darkness. Chico learned to use his machete carefully to cut the bark of the rubber tree. From this cut the milky latex oozed out and dripped down the trunk. Chico caught it in a cup. Each cut produced only a little latex. However, a tree could be cut many times and survive.

The working day was long. Fifteen hours of work

An Indian harvesting rubber. He can do so without killing the tree.

might yield six or eight pounds of raw latex. And the job did not stop there. The latex needed to be smoked over a fire after it was harvested. Raw latex attracted insects and dirt, making it less valuable.

In 1962, when Mendes was eighteen, he met Euclides Fernandes Távora. Távora was from another area and had a university degree. He showed Mendes the first newspaper he had ever seen. Each week Mendes walked three hours through the forest to Távora's hut. There he heard stories of the endless historical struggles between the rich and the poor. Slowly, Mendes developed a political philosophy.

As a full-time tapper, Mendes saw how exploited the tappers were. He had no power or prestige, but he was attracted to their cause. At twenty-two, he began writing letters to the government protesting the tappers' suffering. Why did tappers have to pay rent on trails that needed no upkeep? Why did tappers have to give over their raw latex — and so much of the profits — to middlemen? Why couldn't the tappers sell it directly themselves?

These questions grew out of the long history of rubber in Amazonia. It had been just a curiosity to the first Europeans who found it. The word *rubber* itself came from one of its first uses — "rubbing" off pencil marks in England. Rubberized fabrics were also used to make the first hot-air balloons in 1783. A hundred years later, vulcanized rubber (which was heated with sulfur) became the prime ingredient for making car and bicycle tires.

Harvesting latex had lured thousands of poor men and their families to western Brazil. Between 1850 and 1900, the number of rubber tappers in the Amazon rose from 5,300 to 124,300. These men settled in the forests within walking distance of the rivers. The tappers were in debt from the moment they arrived in the rain forest because they had borrowed the money to make the trip. Plus, they had to buy everything from local stores owned by their bosses, who imposed fees and regulations designed to keep the tappers from ever prospering.

Because they earned so little, the tappers' debts were never paid off. Thousands died every year from diseases and the poor working conditions, but nobody left. The survivors could never afford it.

Chico Mendes' grandfather had been one of those first workers in the rain forest. He had eked out an existence, and so had his son. Chico himself was determined to do better. He wanted to improve his life not just for himself or his family, but for all *seringueiros*.

The letters he wrote to the government did little good, but Mendes did not give up. He stubbornly took another approach. In the early 1970s he began visiting tappers in the area. They were never going to improve things as individuals, he said. They needed to be organized. They needed to speak with one voice. In 1975, Mendes helped set up the first rural trade union in Amazonia.

later she met Chico Mendes, and they began to work together. The 129 tappers who met in Brasília in 1985 represented several different unions. They had traveled hundreds of miles by boat or bus or car. Few could afford to fly. In fact, few could really afford to take the trip at all.

The tappers were not used to working with one another. For many of them, this was the first time they had ever left their villages. But they needed to create a united front.

At the first meeting, the tappers spoke about social justice and workers' rights. They and their families had been cruelly abused for generations. The rubber bosses, the men who owned the land, had taken advantage of their ignorance and fear and the debts they had incurred. Too often the government had ignored the tappers. Sometimes the government had taken advantage of the tappers, too.

The tappers were battling the many forces of development. Twenty years earlier, in 1955, Brazil had begun an ambitious building program. The center of it was their new capital city, Brasília, 600 miles inland from the coast. From Brasília, several highways radiated outward. The first major road through the Amazon was started in 1958. Others followed. Each new one increased the value of the land around it, drawing speculators and other settlers to new areas.

In the 1970s, between 200,000 and 400,000 people moved into the region. The people needed space in which to live, space that was taken up by the rain forest. So the trees were cleared away. In each dry season, the uprooted plant growth was burned to get rid of it.

No tapper could fight all this alone. Even the local unions were severely outnumbered. The tappers needed power and influence. That was why they were meeting.

The forty-year-old Mendes spoke on the second day of the conference. He was not an especially fiery speaker. Physically, he did not command attention. His tousled black hair and mustache were not carefully groomed. His clothes were well-worn. He looked, in fact, much like most of the men he was addressing.

But Mendes was different. He had energy and persistence. He also had a calm manner. He was able to bring people together and get them to resolve their differences.

Unfortunately, 129 tappers, however united, were not going to get very far on their own. Mendes told them the truth. The Brazilian rubber boom had ended in the early twentieth century when rubber trees had been imported to Asia where they could be grown more efficiently. The development of synthetic rubber had also greatly affected the market. Some need for Brazilian rubber remained, but not a large one. Mendes explained that to save their way of life, the tappers would need help. By nature, the tappers were fiercely independent. The time had come, though, to find allies whose interests overlapped their own.

The most likely of these allies were environmentalists. A few months earlier, Mendes had gone to the United States for the first time. He wanted to explore the potential in building alliances with the environmental movement. He and Mary Allegretti had met with government officials, foundation representatives, and members of environmental organizations.

They found they had much in common. The Amazon rain forest had already begun to attract attention worldwide. In just a few hundred years, 15 million square miles of rain forest worldwide had been cut to 6.2 million square miles. The Amazon was a third of that. But as Mendes was quick to point out, much of it was threatened. In the 1970s and 1980s, Brazilian development leveled about ten percent of that third. This was an area roughly the size of Alaska.

The dangers went far beyond simply losing many beautiful trees. Forests are very important to the cycle of life on earth. They cool the planet by absorbing heat from the sun. The chlorophyll in green leaves changes this heat into a form of energy that people and animals can use. This process is called photosynthesis. It uses up carbon dioxide in the air and creates oxygen.

Carbon dioxide is produced every time someone breathes. It is created in large amounts from burning fossil fuels like oil and coal. If carbon dioxide wasn't recycled by plants, too much of it would

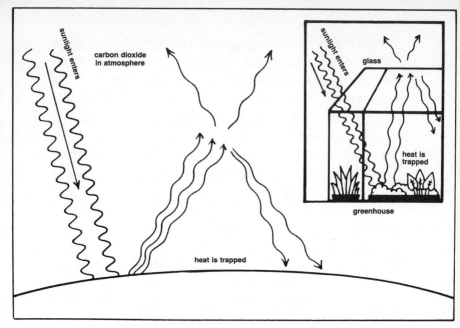

The Greenhouse Effect: Carbon dioxide in the atmosphere acts like the glass in a greenhouse, allowing sunlight to enter. But once the sunlight strikes and warms objects, the heat that those objects give off is trapped inside — prevented from leaking back out into space. The more carbon dioxide in the atmosphere, the more heat is trapped.

build up in the atmosphere. It would continue to let the sun's light in, but it would not let as much heat escape. This combination is good for a greenhouse, but not so good for people. This *greenhouse effect* would raise the earth's temperature. Higher temperatures would change the weather, cause major coastal flooding, and other problems. Since over half of all photosynthesis takes place in the world's forests, maintaining those forests is important.

As Mendes spoke to the tappers, he knew what they were thinking. They did not view themselves as defenders of the forest. Neither had he. But, in fact, that's what they were. On the one hand, Mendes could later say: "I'm not protecting the forest because I'm worried that in twenty years the world will be affected. I'm worried about it because there are thousands of people living here who depend on the forest — and their lives are in danger every day." On the other hand, the tappers had already been environmentally aware. In choosing to prolong the life of trees (rather than just cut them down for the rubber inside), they had always worked in partnership with nature.

Mendes came away from that national meeting with the support of the tappers. But the real battle still lay ahead. The threat to the tappers in western Brazil was more than just a vague government plan. The government, through tax incentives and other measures, had encouraged people to get rich developing the rain forest.

The people who wanted the rain forest cleared were not farmers, but ranchers.

Surprisingly, the rain forest had not turned out to be a source of rich soil. The canopy of the rain forest, the high branches, supported most of the life. Here lived the monkeys, snakes, and birds. The rain forest floor was dark. Only a little sunlight reached it. The soil was thin, and the roots were shallow because everything was drawn upward to the light. Once the land was cleared, that soil was no longer protected from the tropical sun. Within a few years, it dried out.

Tappers and ranchers did not get along. The ranchers saw the value in the land itself. The tappers saw the value in what grew on it. The ranchers, having paid their money, were impatient to see their land cleared. Under Brazilian law, though, anyone who has lived on a plot of land for a year and a day cannot be evicted without compensation. Almost every tapper had these squatter's rights.

Many of the ranchers were not troubled by this apparent stumbling block. They were perfectly willing to use violence if needed. Anyone who protested their actions could get hurt or killed. During the 1970s over 100 people — union organizers, priests, activist lawyers — had been murdered for taking up the tappers' cause. There was even an established pay scale for hired guns. On the low end, a rural union leader could be murdered for a few hundred dollars. A judge or a bishop, though, could cost as much as $20,000. And when people were marked for death, they were always told ahead of time. This death announcement, the *anuncio*, was not given to allow the victim time to run or hide. It was done to be cruel.

One man who fell under an *anuncio* was Wilson Pinheiro. He was a tapper from Brasília who became close friends with Chico Mendes. It was Pineiro who created a stand-off strategy — the *empate* — for dealing with the encroaching ranchers. In an *empate*, fifty or sixty tappers set out to confront peacefully a crew of workers cutting down the forest. Such crews were usually small, perhaps just a dozen men. The tapper leader would explain why the crew should not be cutting. He would ask them to stop. The crews, badly outnumbered, usually agreed. There was always the threat of a fight, but fighting rarely happened. There was nothing to keep a crew from returning. Of course, there was nothing to keep the tappers from returning, either.

Empates weren't always successful. Mendes himself helped to organize forty-five in all. Of those he thought only fifteen had really been successful. But those fifteen had saved over 7 million acres of forest.

Wilson Pinheiro did not live to see the creation of a national organization of tappers. He was killed in July 1980. His friend Chico Mendes might have been killed, too, but he was away on a trip at the time. Even so, Mendes went into hiding for two months until things quieted down.

In 1986, the year after the national tappers organization was created, Mendes witnessed another milestone. With the help of the Brazilian environmentalist José Lutzenberger, Mendes helped set up the Amazonian Alliance of the Peoples of the Forest. This organization merged the resources of the tappers and the native Indians. The forest was home to both, and they shared the same enemies — developers.

For the 200,000 Indians left in the forest, the occupation of the Amazon was just the latest wave of oppression. Most of them had been enslaved or killed by the first Spanish settlers. As late as the 1960s they were still being massacred through poison or disease. Joining with the tappers did not excite them at first. They eventually realized, though, that both groups would benefit.

The next two years were busy ones for Mendes. His home was in Xapuri, a sleepy river town and rubber trading outpost of 5,000 people. Mendes lived there with his second wife Ilzamar, whom he had married in 1983. (His first marriage had ended in divorce.) He was thirty-nine then and she was twenty. Their marriage was strained by their long separations, which often extended for months. Mendes would not let Ilzamar travel with him. He would come home for a few days and then be off again. In August 1986, Ilzamar gave birth to twins, but one died in childbirth.

It was from Xapuri that Mendes began running in 1986 for a seat in the state legislature — and was ultimately defeated. This was the latest of several political defeats. Mendes wouldn't bend his principles to win votes. This integrity was a strength in his union work, but it was a political handicap.

Despite his political defeats, he continued to recruit rubber tappers for his union. Andrew Revkin, in his comprehensive book, *The Burning Season*, described the way Mendes worked:

When Mendes first arrived in a *seringal*, he would not immediately call a meeting. He would walk up to the house of an individual tapper and sit for a while. After taking a tin cup of water, he would ask the tapper about his life, his situation. Mendes would play with the children as he sat, admiring the construction of the house or the quality of the manioc growing nearby. He would try to learn about that one tapper's problems. . . . Only after he had personally gained the trust of each tapper would he start talking about the union, about organizing, about resistance.

One outsider who was impressed with Mendes was the British documentary filmmaker Adrian Cowell. He filmed much of Mendes' work from 1986 on. Cowell had worked in the Amazon for many years. He was very concerned about the destruction of the rain forest. The tappers' struggle, he thought, had the potential to save the rain forest, but only if that struggle received international attention.

Cowell thought Chico Mendes could take the tappers' message onto a wider stage. Mendes spoke plainly and clearly. "He talked to everybody the same way," Cowell would later remember, "and listened to everybody's side, and slowly brought all the different factions together."

The need for a wider stage was becoming more and more evident. On September 9, 1987, an orbiting satellite detected a record 7,603 different fires burning in the Amazon. In that year alone, 48,000 square miles of forest (an area the size of Pennsylvania) went up in smoke. Over 300,000

A recently destroyed forest in Brazil.

square miles had been cleared since 1975. And it wasn't just the loss of the rain forest that concerned environmentalists. These Amazon fires were releasing millions of tons of carbon monoxide, soot, and harmful gases — as much pollution as some European countries were putting out in the same year.

The battle had passed the point of improving working conditions for the tappers. Good working conditions wouldn't help them if there was no longer any forest to work in. The tappers needed a legal framework to give them control of their land.

It was Mendes who came up with the idea that became known as the extractive reserve. He was later interviewed about its history. "Until 1984," he said, "we were doing *empates* but we didn't have much clarity about what we wanted. We knew that deforestation was the end of us all and all the living beings of the forest. But the thing stopped there. People said, do you want to stop the deforestation to transform Amazonia into a sanctuary? Make it untouchable? There was the impasse."

Under his extractive reserve plan, the tappers would not own the land. The government would buy it. But the tappers would have the right to harvest, or extract, rubber, nuts, and other products from it. A study had shown that a family of tappers and nut gatherers could make $1,333 a year, while farmers made $800 and ranchers $710. Clearly, the forest could be put to work at a profit without threatening its survival.

In 1987, with the helpful lobbying of Mary Allegretti, legislation allowing the reserves was signed into law. This was a far-reaching achievement for the tappers. There were no guarantees that the government would appropriate the funds, but the momentum was heading that way.

The swirl of events was moving faster and faster for Mendes. With his friends in environmental circles — Mary Allegretti, José Lutzenberger, and Adrian Cowell — recommending him, Mendes won two international awards. From the United Nations Environmental Program, he received one of the Global 500 Awards, which was given to leaders in conservation and the environment. From the Better World Society he received the Protection of the Environment Medal.

When Mendes won his awards, few Brazilian reporters knew who he was. Abroad, however, he was becoming a symbol of the endangered rain forest. In 1987 he went to Miami, Florida, to speak at a conference. Many American banks were financing roads through the Amazon, thinking to help the local economy. The environmental and social impact of these roads was rarely considered. Mendes explained the harm these roads were doing. The bankers listened, and many changed their policies.

This success, the awards, and new grants from foundations all increased Mendes' prestige in Brazil. They also made him a more important target. Mendes had made many enemies over the years. The most dangerous of them was the Alves family. Darly Alves da Silva had a 10,000-acre ranch outside Xapuri. He and his sons were not very hardworking ranchers. It was thought that they made their money doing the "dirty work" for other ranchers, and they did their own dirty work, too — several unsolved (and mostly uninvestigated) murders were alleged to be their handiwork.

The Alves family threatened Mendes many times. Their greatest confrontation came in the town of Cachoeira. It was the source of his strongest support and his childhood home. The Alveses had bought some of the Seringal Cachoeira. They were not really interested in developing this rubber plantation. They just wanted to clear the land and sell it to somebody else.

Mendes was determined to keep this from happening. He organized a large *empate* of rubber tappers and their families. The Alveses had a chainsaw crew protected by off-duty military police, but the *empate* worked. There were just too many tappers to deal with.

It was a victory for Mendes. But it made him the bitter enemy of Darly Alves and his sons. Mendes had made them look foolish. He could not be allowed to do that.

In early June of 1988, Mendes went to Rio de Janeiro for some speaking engagements and interviews. His friends hoped that his growing reputation in the outside world would somehow protect him when he returned home to Xapuri.

On October 8, 1988, Seringal Cachoeira became an extractive reserve. The government had bought the land. It was safe now, far safer than Chico Mendes himself. The creation of this reserve worried the ranchers. If too much land became extractive reserves, it would affect the value of what was left. The ranchers had already tried to buy Mendes off. He had refused their bribes, though — even though he was a poor man. Now they would have to take further steps.

By the end of October, the casual threats against him had been replaced with death pronouncements. Although the discovery of an old murder-related warrant against Darly Alves and his brother had forced them into hiding, they were only out of sight, not gone for good. Some of Mendes' friends and family thought he should leave Xapuri for a while. But he refused: "I would be a coward to do this. My blood is the same blood as that of these people suffering here. I can't run. There's something inside me that cannot leave here. This is the place where I will finish my mission."

Mendes tried to be careful. He had bodyguards, and he took precautions. But it was hard, day after day, to question every move he made in terms of his personal safety. The continual watchfulness was wearing down his sense of caution.

On December 22, 1988, Mendes walked out his back door to take a shower. He was shot several times from the shadows. The killer or killers ran off at once. Ilzamar ran to her husband's side, but there was nothing she or anyone else could do.

The death of Chico Mendes did not signal the defeat of the tappers. More than a thousand local people attended his funeral. The murder drew worldwide attention. Under the glare of the international spotlight, the Brazilian government attempted a major investigation. Finally, Darly Alves confessed to the crime. Much confusion remained, though, about whether he had acted alone.

Although the case did not go to trial until late 1990, the government acted in the meantime to further the tappers' cause. The union had continued its work and new leaders were emerging. Earlier that year, the Chico Mendes Reserve was created. It covered almost every area Mendes personally had ever fought for. Other reserves were also created, totaling close to 10,000 square miles. More are on the way.

It is an appropriate legacy for Chico Mendes.

Ilzamar Mendes with a photo of her late husband.

He had become the leader of the tappers because their welfare was a concern he could not ignore. When their need grew into a larger environmental movement, he accepted that, too. As he once said, "We started fighting for the rubber tree and Brazil nut tree and the good little life we had in the forest. And then we discovered that we were defending the whole of Amazonia. And now I have come to realize that what we are fighting for is all of humanity."

Bibliography

John Muir

Adams, Alexander B. *The Disputed Lands*. New York: G.P. Putnam's Sons, 1981.

Cleland, Robert Glass. *From Wilderness to Empire: A History of California*, ed. Glenn S. Dumke. New York: Alfred A. Knopf, 1962.

Fox, Stephen. *John Muir and His Legacy: The American Conservation Movement*. Boston: Little, Brown and Company, 1981.

Haines, Madge, and Leslie Morrill. *John Muir, Protector of the Wilds*. New York: Abingdon Press, 1957.

Lavender, David. *The American Heritage History of the Great West*. New York: American Heritage Publishing Company, 1965.

Paul, Rodman W. *The Far West and the Great Plains in Transition 1859–1900*. New York: Harper & Row, 1988.

Silverberg, Robert. *John Muir*. New York: G.P. Putnam's Sons, 1972.

Starr, Kevin. *Americans and the California Dream 1850–1915*. New York: Oxford University Press, 1973.

Williams, Richard L. *The Loggers*. New York: Time-Life Books, 1976.

Winther, Oscar O. *The Transportation Frontier*. New York: Holt, Rinehart and Winston, 1964.

Rachel Carson

Brooks, Paul. *The House of Life: Rachel Carson at Work*. Boston: Houghton Mifflin Company, 1972.

Carson, Rachel. *The Sea Around Us*. New York: Oxford University Press, 1961.

Carson, Rachel. *The Sense of Wonder*. New York: Harper & Row, 1965.

Carson, Rachel. *Silent Spring*. Boston: Houghton Mifflin Company, 1962.

Graham, Frank Jr. *Since Silent Spring*. Boston: Houghton Mifflin Company, 1970.

Hirsch, S. Carl. *Guardians of Tomorrow*. New York: Viking, 1971.

Jezer, Marty. *Rachel Carson*. New York: Chelsea House, 1988.

Lauwerys, J.A. *Man's Impact on Nature*. Garden City, New York: The Natural History Press, 1970.

Rudd, Robert L. *Pesticides and the Living Landscape*. Madison, WI: The University of Wisconsin Press, 1964.

Sterling, Philip. *Sea and Earth: The Life of Rachel Carson*. New York: Thomas Y. Crowell Company, 1970.

Lois Gibbs

Brown, Michael. *Laying Waste: The Poisoning of America by Toxic Chemicals*. New York: Pantheon, 1979.

Ehrlich, Paul R., and Anne H. Ehrlich. *Earth*. New York: Franklin Watts, 1987.

Epstein, Samuel S., Lester O. Brown and Carl Pope. *Hazardous Waste in America*. San Francisco: Sierra Club Books, 1982.

Gibbs, Lois Marie. *My Story*. Albany, NY: State University of New York Press, 1982.

Kiefer, Irene. *Poisoned Land: The Problem of Hazardous Waste*. New York: Atheneum, 1981.

Krensky, Stephen. Interview with Lois Gibbs, January 4, 1991.

Levine, Adeline Gordon. *Love Canal: Science, Politics and People*. Lexington, MA: D.C. Heath and Company, Lexington Books, 1982.

Trost, Cathy. *Elements of Risk*. New York: Times Books, 1984.

Whelan, Elizabeth. *Toxic Terror*. Ottawa, IL: Jameson Books, 1985.

Zipko, Stephen J. *Toxic Threat*. New York: Julian Messner, 1986.

Chico Mendes

Cowell, Adrian. *The Decade of Destruction*. New York: Henry Holt and Company, 1990.

Dubos René. *The Wooing of Earth*. New York: Scribners, 1980.

Hecht, Susanna, and Alexander Cockburn. *The Fate of the Forest*. London: Verso, 1989.

Mathews, Tom. "A Life Under Fire in Brazil." *Newsweek* (September 3, 1990) pp. 62–64.

Revkin, Andrew. *The Burning Season*. Boston: Houghton Mifflin, 1990.

Shoumatoff, Alex. *The World Is Burning*. Boston: Little, Brown, 1990.

Time-Life Books. *Brazil*. Amsterdam, The Netherlands: Time-Life Books, 1986.

Index

Road construction, Amazon rain forest and, 92
Roosevelt, Theodore, and Muir, John, 25
Rubber, cultivation of, 82; history of, 79
Rubber tappers, cattle industry and, 86; environmental awareness of, 85; extractive reserve plan and, 91, 95; health and, 80; Indians and, 88; Mendes, Chico and, 77–82; organization of, 79, 80–81, 82–83, 89; rain forest protection and, 86–87

San Francisco, California, growth of, 6; Muir, John and, 9; population of, 6; water needs of, 25, 27
Santa Clara Valley, California, 10
Science, social change and, 29–30
Scotland, 7
Seattle, Washington, 19
Senate. *See* United States Congress.
Sequoia National Park, establishment of, 23
Seringal Cachoeira, Brazil, 93
Seringueiros. *See* Rubber tappers.
Shawn, William, 38
Sheep, 11
Sierra Club, creation of, 24; Muir, John and, 24, 25
Silent Spring (Carson), 42–48
Skinker, Mary, 33
Sludge, hazardous wastes and, 57
Southern Pacific Railroad, 23
Soviet Union, nuclear test ban treaty, 52–53
Spanish conquistadors, Amazon and, 75
Steamships, 2
Steel industry, pollution and, 32
Strentzel, John, 16–17
Strother, Robert S., 39
Sun, rain forests and, 83–84

Sutter's Mill, California, 5

Távora, Euclides Fernandes, 77–78
Technology, social change and, 29–30
Telephone, 29
Texas, annexation of, 5
Transcontinental railroad, construction of, 14. *See also* Railroads.
Transportation, westward movement and, 6–7. *See also* Airplane; Automobile; Railroads.

Union of Soviet Socialist Republics, nuclear test ban treaty, 52–53
Union Pacific Railroad, construction of, 14
United Kingdom, nuclear test ban treaty, 52–53
United Nations Environmental Program, 92
United States Bureau of Fisheries, 34
United States Congress, Carson, Rachel and, 49; Environmental Protection Agency (EPA) created by, 54; hazardous wastes and, 57; Homestead Act of 1862, 14, 16; national park system and, 21; pesticides and, 48; railroads and, 14; Yosemite Valley and, 9, 23
United States Fish and Wildlife Service, 34

Velsicol Chemical Corporation, 42, 44
Voting rights, women, 33

Wagon trains, 6
Weedkillers, dangers to food chain of, 36; development of, 30
Westward movement, gold rush and, 5; promoters and, 13; transportation and, 6–7

About the Author

STEPHEN KRENSKY is the author of more than thirty books for children, including *George Washington: The Man Who Would Not Be King* and *Children of the Earth and Sky* for Scholastic. He lives in Lexington, Massachusetts, with his wife, Joan, and their sons, Andrew and Peter.

SCHOLASTIC BIOGRAPHY

Available wherever you buy books, or use this order form.

Scholastic Inc., P.O. Box 7502, 2931 East McCarty Street, Jefferson City, MO 65102

Please send me the books I have checked above. I am enclosing $_____ (please add $2.00 to cover shipping and handling). Send check or money order — no cash or C.O.D.s please.

Name_____ Birthdate _____

Address_____

City_____ State/Zip _____

Please allow four to six weeks for delivery. Available in the U.S. only. Sorry, mail orders are not available to residents of Canada. Prices subject to change.   BIO695

APPLE® PAPERBACKS

Pick an Apple and Polish Off Some Great Reading!

BEST-SELLING APPLE TITLES

❑ MT43944-8	**Afternoon of the Elves** Janet Taylor Lisle	**$2.99**
❑ MT41624-3	**The Captive** Joyce Hansen	**$3.50**
❑ MT43266-4	**Circle of Gold** Candy Dawson Boyd	**$3.50**
❑ MT44064-0	**Class President** Johanna Hurwitz	**$3.50**
❑ MT45436-6	**Cousins** Virginia Hamilton	**$3.50**
❑ MT43130-7	**The Forgotten Door** Alexander Key	**$2.95**
❑ MT44569-3	**Freedom Crossing** Margaret Goff Clark	**$3.50**
❑ MT42858-6	**Hot and Cold Summer** Johanna Hurwitz	**$3.50**
❑ MT25514-2	**The House on Cherry Street 2: The Horror**	
	Rodman Philbrick and Lynn Harnett	**$3.50**
❑ MT41708-8	**The Secret of NIMH** Robert C. O'Brien	**$3.99**
❑ MT42882-9	**Sixth Grade Sleepover** Eve Bunting	**$3.50**
❑ MT42537-4	**Snow Treasure** Marie McSwigan	**$3.50**
❑ MT42378-9	**Thank You, Jackie Robinson** Barbara Cohen	**$3.99**

Available wherever you buy books, or use this order form

Scholastic Inc., P.O. Box 7502, 2931 East McCarty Street, Jefferson City, MO 65102

Please send me the books I have checked above. I am enclosing $_____ (please add $2.00 to cover shipping and handling). Send check or money order—no cash or C.O.D.s please.

Name_____**Birthdate**_____

Address_____

City_____**State/Zip**_____

Please allow four to six weeks for delivery. Offer good in U.S. only. Sorry mail orders are not available to residents of Canada. Prices subject to change.   APP596